D0600624

Sports Dream

Parent's Introduction

Welcome to **We Read Phonics**! This series is designed to help you assist your child in reading. Each book includes a story, as well as some simple word games to play with your child. The games focus on the phonics skills and sight words your child will use in reading the story.

Here are some recommendations for using this book with your child:

1 Word Play

There are word games both before and after the story. Make these games fun and playful. If your child becomes bored or frustrated, play a different game or take a break.

Phonics is a method of sounding out words by blending together letter sounds. However, not all words can be "sounded out." **Sight words** are frequently used words that usually cannot be sounded out.

2 Read the Story

After some word play, read the story aloud to your child—or read the story together, by reading aloud at the same time or by taking turns. As you and your child read, move your finger under the words.

Next, have your child read the entire story to you while you follow along with your finger under the words. If there is some difficulty with a word, either help your child to sound it out or wait about five seconds and then say the word.

3 Discuss and Read Again

After reading the story, talk about it with your child. Ask questions like, "What happened in the story?" and "What was the best part?" It will be helpful for your child to read this story to you several times. Another great way for your child to practice is by reading the book to a younger sibling, a pet, or even a stuffed animal!

It was so cool when he was racing the dirt bike!

LEVEL 5 **Level 5** introduces words with "ai" and "ay" with the long "a" sound (as in *bait* and *day*), "igh," "y," and "ie" with the long "i" sound (as in *high, cry,* and *tied*), and the "ng" sound (as in *song* and *king*). Also included are the word endings -er and -ing (as in *higher* and *running*).

Sports Dream

A We Read Phonics™ Book
Level 5

Text Copyright © 2011 by Treasure Bay, Inc.
Illustrations Copyright © 2011 by Jeffrey Ebbeler

Reading Consultants: Bruce Johnson, M.Ed., and Dorothy Taguchi, Ph.D.

We Read Phonics™ is a trademark of Treasure Bay, Inc.

4732 3505 10/11

Published by
Treasure Bay, Inc.
P.O. Box 119
Novato, CA 94948 USA

Printed in Singapore

Library of Congress Catalog Card Number: 2010932588

Hardcover ISBN: 978-1-60115-335-7
Paperback ISBN: 978-1-60115-336-4

We Read Phonics™
Patent Pending

Visit us online at:
www.TreasureBayBooks.com

PR-11-10

Sports Dream

By Paul Orshoski

Illustrated by Jeffrey Ebbeler

Making Words

Creating words with these letter combinations will help your child read the words in this story.

Materials: thick paper or cardboard; pencil, crayon, or marker; scissors

1. Cut 2 x 2 inch squares from the paper or cardboard and print these letters and letter combinations on the squares: ai, ay, igh, ie, ing, y, g, n, s, l, b, t, m, d, p, h, k, c, and r.

2. Place the cards letter side up in front of your child.

3. Ask your child to make and say words using the letters available. For example, your child could choose the letters "g," "ai," and "n," and make the word *gain.*

4. If your child has difficulty, try presenting letters that will make a specific word. For example, present "s," "ai," and "l," and ask your child to make *sail.* You could then ask your child to find a letter to change the word to *mail.*

5. Ask your child to make as many words as possible that use the "ai," "ay," "igh," and "y" cards. These letter patterns are used in the story. Possible words include *gain, sail, stain, bait, aim, day, play, pay, high, might, sky, cry, try,* and *lie.*

Memory

This is a fun way to practice recognizing some sight words used in the story.

1 Write each word listed on the right on two plain 3 x 5 inch cards, so you have two sets of cards. Using one set of cards, ask your child to repeat each word after you. Shuffle both decks of cards together, and place them face down on a flat surface.

2 The first player turns over one card and says the word, then turns over a second card and says the word. If the cards match, the player takes those cards and continues to play. If they don't match, both cards are turned over, and it's the next player's turn.

3 Keep the cards. You can make more cards with other **We Read Phonics** books and combine the cards for even bigger games!

little

over

around

look

would

some

all

before

only

T1-BLC-995

3

I dream all day of little things
when I go out to play.

I dream I am a high-speed champ
and making lots of pay.

I long to ride a dirt bike . . .

. . . and win a big, huge race.

Yet when I ride, I often crash
and flip and plant my face.

To star at playing basketball
would be the best wish yet.

For such a thing to happen,
my shots must reach the net.

I think of leaping over cliffs
to sail around the sky.

Yet when I look before I leap,
I just turn white and cry.

I dream of playing soccer
with grass stains on my shirt.

Yet when I try, I bop my top
and lie face down in dirt.

I dream of playing hardball
and batting balls with glee.

Yet when I swing, I seem to miss.
The ump yells out, "Strike three!"

I dream of going fishing
to reel some big fish in.

Yet all I do is drop my bait
and then I take a swim.

I hope to bang a puck on ice
and be the best in state.

The only problem I can see
is that I cannot skate.

I aim to golf just like a pro
and make a hole in one.

But all my strokes go off the mark,
and then I need to run.

At playing sports my skills fall short.
I do the best I can.

And while I am no super star, . . .

. . . I am a super fan.

Picture Walk Review

Would you like to try reading this page again?

Help your child to review challenging words, as well as to reread and discuss the story.

1. Turn to a page where your child had some difficulty. Point to the challenging words and ask your child to read them. Then ask your child to read the page again. Talk about the picture on the page.

2. Turn to a page where your child seemed to enjoy the story. Discuss the picture. Discuss what your child enjoyed about that part of the story.

3. Continue "walking" through the story, asking questions about the pictures or the story. Encourage discussion.

4. Encourage your child to read the story again.